SLIDES, FLIPS, AND TURNS

Claire Piddock

Crabtree Publishing Company

www.crabtreebooks.com

Author: Claire Piddock
Publishing plan research and development:
  Sean Charlebois, Reagan Miller
  Crabtree Publishing Company
Editor: Molly Aloian
Editorial director: Kathy Middleton
Project coordinator: Margaret Salter
Prepress technician: Margaret Salter
Coordinating editor: Chester Fisher
Series editor: Jessica Cohn
Project manager: Kumar Kunal (Q2AMEDIA)
Art direction: Rahul Dhiman (Q2AMEDIA)
Cover design: Shruti Aggarwal (Q2AMEDIA)
Design: Cheena Yadav (Q2AMEDIA)
Photo research: Poulomi Basu (Q2AMEDIA)

Photographs:
Shutterstock: Jackhollingsworthcom LLC/David Davis: front cover
Photolibrary: Walter Bibikow: front cover
Q2AMedia Image Bank: title page, p. 5, p. 9, p. 13
Q2AMedia Art Bank: p. 4, p. 6, p. 7, p. 8, p. 9, p. 10, p. 11, p. 13, p. 14, p. 15,
  p. 16, p. 17, p. 18, p. 19, p. 20, p. 21, p. 23

Library and Archives Canada Cataloguing in Publication

Piddock, Claire
  Slides, flips, and turns / Claire Piddock.

(My path to math)
Includes index.
ISBN 978-0-7787-5251-6 (bound).--ISBN 978-0-7787-5298-1 (pbk.)

  1. Geometry--Juvenile literature. 2. Shapes--Juvenile literature.
3. Transformations (Mathematics)--Juvenile literature. I. Title.
II. Series: My path to math

QA445.5.P53 2009   j516'.1   C2009-905367-5

Library of Congress Cataloging-in-Publication Data

Piddock, Claire.
  Slides, flips, and turns / Claire Piddock.
    p. cm. -- (My path to math)
  Includes index.
  ISBN 978-0-7787-5251-6 (reinforced lib. bdg. : alk. paper) -- ISBN 978-0-7787-
5298-1 (pbk. : alk. paper)
  1. Geometry--Juvenile literature. 2. Shapes--Juvenile literature. 3.
Transformations (Mathematics)--Juvenile literature. I. Title. II. Series.

  QA445.5.P476 2010
  516'.1--dc22
                                                          2009035498

Crabtree Publishing Company

Printed in China/122009/CT20090903

www.crabtreebooks.com   1-800-387-7650

Published in Canada
Crabtree Publishing
616 Welland Ave.
St. Catharines, ON
L2M 5V6

Published in the United States
Crabtree Publishing
PMB 59051
350 Fifth Avenue, 59th Floor
New York, New York 10118

Published in the United Kingdom
Crabtree Publishing
Maritime House
Basin Road North, Hove
BN41 1WR

Published in Australia
Crabtree Publishing
386 Mt. Alexander Rd.
Ascot Vale (Melbourne)
VIC 3032

Contents

Happy Birthday!

Soon it will be Grandma's birthday! Sofia wants to make her a birthday card. Sofia's mom helps gather materials. They look for shapes to put along the borders of the card.

They move the shapes in different ways to see how the shapes look. Sofia's mom tells her about **transformations**. The different ways a shape can be moved on a flat surface are called transformations.

Activity Box

Which shape would you choose for a border? Why?

circle   heart   square   flower   triangle   hat

They fold paper to make a card. Then they decorate it with shapes.

Slides

A **slide** is one kind of transformation. A slide moves a shape in a straight line in any direction.

Sofia decides to use hearts on the front of the card. She places a heart in the middle. She slides the shape in many directions to see where it looks best. Then she pastes heart shapes around the border. Sofia likes how the card looks.

slide to the right   slide to the left   slide up   slide down   slide **diagonally**

Activity Box

You can show slides by sliding around on your feet! Slide forward. Slide backward. Slide to the left. Slide to the right.

Happy Birthday

Sofia's card is taking shape!

Flips

Mom shows Sofia a **flip**. A flip moves a shape across a line so the shape faces another direction. The line can be real or imagined. The line can be in different directions.

A flip over a **vertical** line moves an object to the side.

   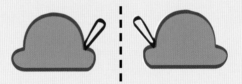

A flip over a **horizontal** line moves an object up and down.

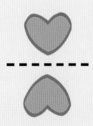   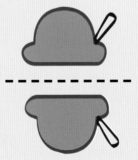

Activity Box

A flip is like a reflection in a mirror. Write GRANDMA on a piece of paper. See what it looks like when shown in a mirror.

A heart looks the same after a flip to the side. It does not look the same after a flip down!

More Flips

Grandma's name is Linda. Her name starts with an L. Mom asks, "What happens when you flip an L sideways?"

Sofia tries flipping an L sideways, over a vertical line. Then she tries flipping an L up and down over a horizontal line. She decides to use flips of the letter L for the border of the second page of her card.

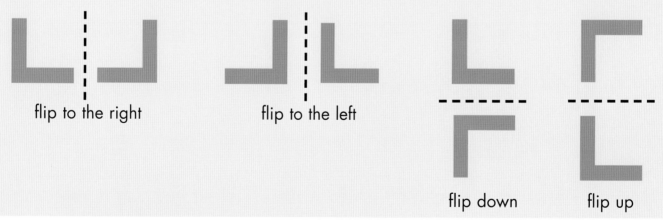

flip to the right

flip to the left

flip down

flip up

Activity Box

What does the first letter of your name look like when you flip it each way? You can also use shapes to explore flips.

Love

A flip is also called a reflection.

Turns

Mom tells Sofia that a **turn** is another type of transformation. A turn moves an object around a center **point**. A turn is also called a rotation.

A turn works like the hands moving around a clock. Mom draws an arrow pointing right. Then she draws an arrow pointing down. "These arrows show a **quarter turn**," she says.

"Here is a **half turn**," says Mom. She draws an arrow pointing right followed by an arrow in the opposite direction.

Activity Box

A quarter turn of the big hand of a clock shows that a quarter of an hour has passed. A half turn means half an hour has passed. What does a **full turn** of the big hand show?

▲ quarter turn

▲ half turn

Sofia pretends that her arms are the hands of a clock!

More Turns

Sofia likes making turns with the shapes.
She tries turns with a heart.

quarter turn   half turn   **three-quarter turn**   full turn

Then she makes turns with the letter S, for Sofia.

quarter turn   half turn   three-quarter turn   full turn

She tries turning a flower, too.

quarter turn   half turn   three-quarter turn   full turn

Activity Box

The S looks the same after a half turn.
Will a square look the same after a half
turn? What about the letter L?

14

Flowers for you from Sofia

Sofia uses flowers for the third page of Grandma's card.

Shape Game

Mom wants to play a game. She will show a shape before and after a transformation. Sofia will say if the shape shows a slide, a flip, or a turn.

They start with a triangle. Sofia says, "A turn!" She is right. They try another shape.

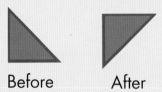

Before   After

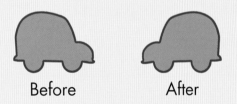

Before   After

"The car is flipped to the left," says Sofia. She is right again. Then they try a harder one.

Before   After

The hat looks the same. But Sofia is not fooled. The hat shape shows a slide. It also shows a full turn!

Activity Box

Use an index card as your shape. Try a flip, a turn, and a slide. Try a combination of moves to see what happens.

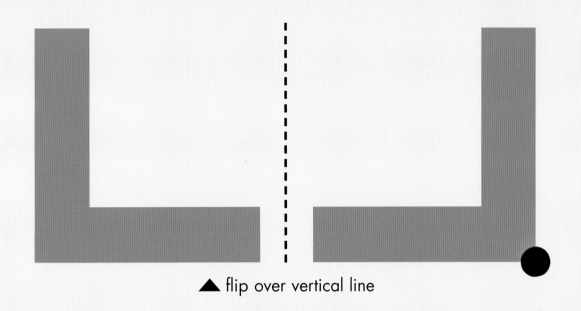

▲ flip over vertical line

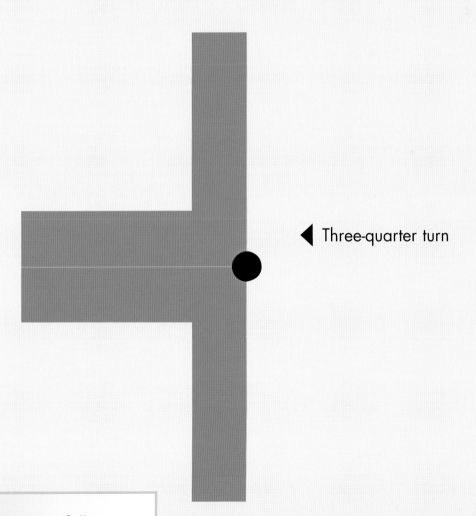

◀ Three-quarter turn

One transformation can follow another. Look at the flip of the L at the top. It is followed by a turn.

Make a Design

Mom shows Sofia how to make a **design** using a combination of slides, flips, and turns.

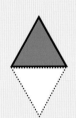
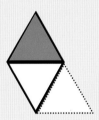
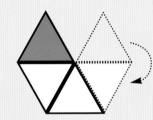

She traces a triangle.

Then she flips it down

She slides it diagonally.

She flips it to the right, then moves it a half turn.

Then Mom makes a design called a **tessellation**. A tessellation is made from shapes that repeat on a flat surface. The shapes do not overlap. There are no spaces between the shapes.

Sofia colors the design.

Activity Box

Trace this shape. Cut it out. Slide it each way and trace it. Make a design that you can color.

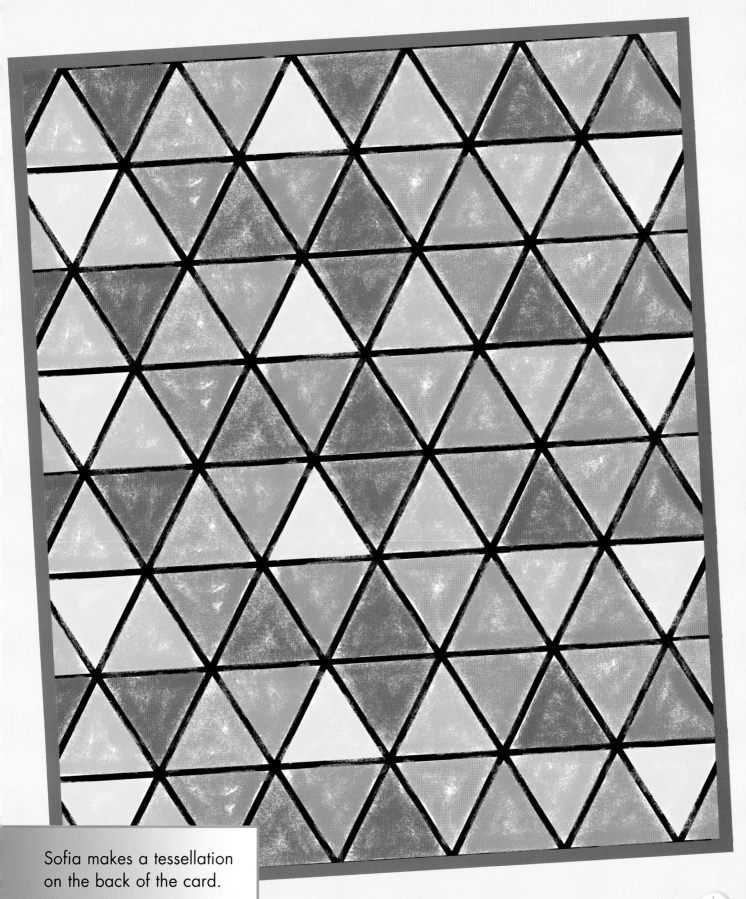

Sofia makes a tessellation on the back of the card.

Moving Shapes

The birthday card is done! Sofia used slides, flips, and turns on each page. Artists use basic shapes and move them in different ways to make designs. They use math. You can, too!

A slide moves a shape in a straight line in any direction.

A flip moves a shape over a line. It is like a reflection in a mirror.

A turn moves a shape around a point.

   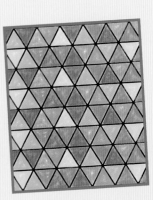

The pictures below show different kinds of transformations.

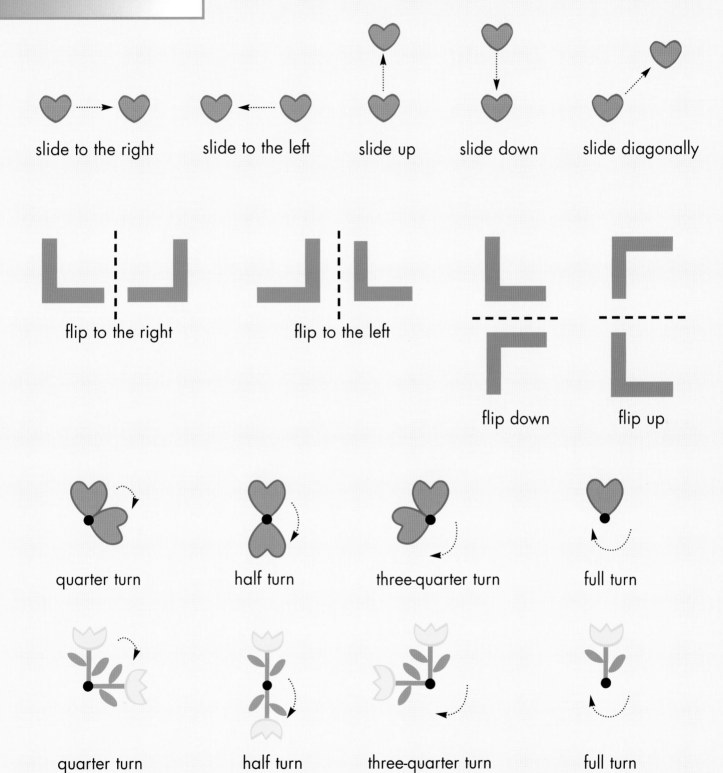

slide to the right   slide to the left   slide up   slide down   slide diagonally

flip to the right   flip to the left

flip down   flip up

quarter turn   half turn   three-quarter turn   full turn

quarter turn   half turn   three-quarter turn   full turn

Glossary

design Planned pattern or arrangement

diagonally In a slanted direction

flip Movement of a shape over a line so the left and right sides or tops and bottoms switch places

full turn Turn that moves all the way around a point, so the shape ends up in the same place

half turn Turn that moves halfway around a point

horizontal Going left and right, as in a line that seems to lie down

point In math, something that has a place but goes nowhere else

quarter turn Turn that moves one-fourth of the way around a point

slide Movement of a shape to a new position along a straight line, without flipping or turning it

tessellation Design made of repeated shapes on a flat surface with no overlaps and no spaces

three-quarter turn Turn that moves three-fourths of the way around a point

transformations Movement of a shape by slides, flips, or turns

turn Movement of a shape to a new position by rotating the figure around a point

vertical Going up and down, as in a line that seems to stand up

Index